S0-ABB-319

JUSTIN TIMBERLAKE

Gareth Stevens
Publishing

By Max Maimone

Please visit our Web site, www.garethstevens.com. For a free color catalog of all our high-quality books, call toll free 1-800-542-2595 or fax 1-877-542-2596.

Library of Congress Cataloging-in-Publication Data

Maimone, Max Q.
  Justin Timberlake / Max Q. Maimone.
      p. cm. — (Hip-hop headliners)
  Includes index.
  ISBN 978-1-4339-4800-8 (library binding)
  ISBN 978-1-4339-4801-5 (pbk.)
  ISBN 978-1-4339-4802-2 (6-pack)
  1. Timberlake, Justin, 1981—Juvenile literature. 2. Singers—United States—Biography—Juvenile literature. I. Title.
  ML3930.T58M35 2011
  782.42164092—dc22
  [B]
                            2010026218

First Edition

Published in 2011 by
Gareth Stevens Publishing
111 East 14th Street, Suite 349
New York, NY 10003

Designer: Haley W. Harasymiw
Editor: Therese Shea

Photo credits: Cover, pp. 2–32 (background) Shutterstock.com; cover (Justin Timberlake), p. 1 Dimitrios Kambouris/Film Magic; pp. 5, 13 Brenda Chase/Getty Images; pp. 7, 25 Kevin Winter/Getty Images; pp. 9, 17 Scott Gries/ImageDirect/Getty Images; p. 11 Lawrence Lucier/Getty Images; p. 15 Getty Images; p. 19 Paul Drinkwater/NBC/Getty Images; p. 21 Arnold Turner/Wire Images; p. 23 Frederick M. Brown/Getty Images; p. 27 Elisabetta Villa/Getty Images; p. 29 Neilson Barnard/Getty Images.

Printed in the United States of America

CPSIA compliance information: Batch #CW11GS: For further information contact Gareth Stevens, New York, New York at 1-800-542-2595.

Contents

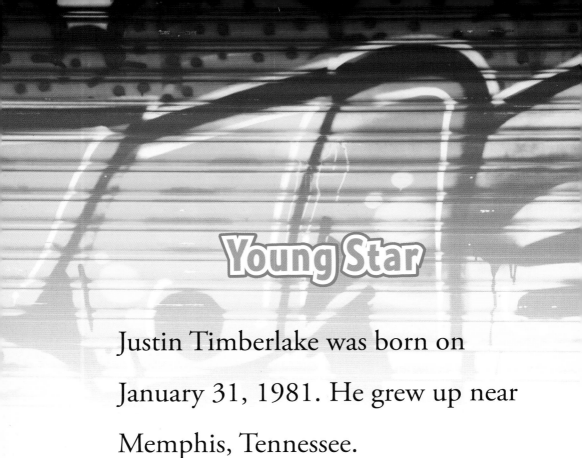

Young Star

Justin Timberlake was born on January 31, 1981. He grew up near Memphis, Tennessee.

In 1989, Justin sang in a contest.
The girls went wild! He was just
8 years old.

In 1992, Justin appeared on the TV show *Star Search*. He sang a love song. He didn't win the contest.

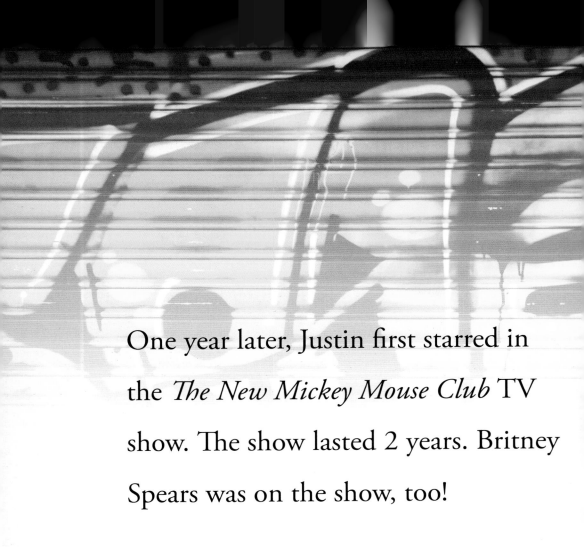

One year later, Justin first starred in the *The New Mickey Mouse Club* TV show. The show lasted 2 years. Britney Spears was on the show, too!

Britney Spears

Getting *NSYNC

In 1995, Justin was picked to be in a music group called *NSYNC. Four other boys sang and danced with him.

Lance Bass

Joey Fatone

Chris Kirkpatrick

J. C. Chasez

13

*NSYNC was a huge hit all over the world. "Tearin' Up My Heart" was one of their first songs.

*NSYNC's second album came out in 2000. It was called *No Strings Attached*. It was the fastest-selling album ever!

Justin Solo

In 2002, Justin put out a solo album. It was called *Justified*. "Like I Love You" and "Cry Me a River" were two hit songs on the album.

In 2003, Justin went on tour with Christina Aguilera. People loved his dance moves!

Christina Aguilera

21

Justin's second solo album was a huge hit as well. He won two Grammys for the album in 2008.

Justin has worked with many hip-hop stars, such as the Black Eyed Peas, Timbaland, Nelly, and Snoop Dogg.

Timbaland

25

Acting and More

Justin is an actor, too. He was the voice of Prince Artie Pendragon in two *Shrek* movies.

Justin and Trace Ayala have a clothing business called William Rast. It is named after their grandfathers. Justin has so many talents!

make.believe

Trace Ayala

29

Timeline

1981   Justin Timberlake is born on January 31.

1993   Justin begins 2 years on *The New Mickey Mouse Club*.

1995   Justin and four others form the group *NSYNC.

2000   *NSYNC's *No Strings Attached* becomes the fastest-selling album.

2002   Justin puts out his first solo album, *Justified*.

2005   Justin and Trace Ayala begin the William Rast clothing business.

2008   Justin wins two Grammys for his second solo album.